A Day's Grace

Poems 1997–2002

Other Books by Robyn Sarah

Poetry

Shadowplay (1978)

The Space Between Sleep and Waking (1981)

Three Sestinas (1984)

Anyone Skating On That Middle Ground (1984)

Becoming Light (1987)

The Touchstone: Poems New and Selected (1992)

Questions About The Stars (1998)

Short Stories

A Nice Gazebo (1992)

Promise of Shelter (1997)

Robyn Sarah
A Day's Grace

Poems 1997–2002

The Porcupine's Quill

National Library of Canada Cataloguing in Publication Data

Sarah, Robyn, 1949–
A day's grace: poems 1997–2002/Robyn Sarah

ISBN 0-88984-233-7

I. Title.

PS8587.A7D39 2003   C811'.54   C2003-905325-3

1 2 3 4 • 05 04 03

Published by The Porcupine's Quill, 68 Main St., Erin, ON NOB 1TO.
www.sentex.net/~pql

Readied for the press by Eric Ormsby; copy edited by Doris Cowan.

Represented in Canada by the Literary Press Group.
Trade orders are available from University of Toronto Press.

We acknowledge the support of the Ontario Arts Council and the
Canada Council for the Arts for our publishing program. The financial
support of the Government of Canada through the Book Publishing
Industry Development Program is also gratefully acknowledged.
Thanks, also, to the Government of Ontario through the Ontario
Media Development Corporation's Ontario Book Initiative.

Canada Council   Conseil des Arts
for the Arts   du Canada

Canadä

ONTARIO ARTS COUNCIL
CONSEIL DES ARTS DE L'ONTARIO

Table of Contents

Here as I pause to greet the day
And raise the sun-flushed blind,
The thought of you, I know not why,
Comes stealing to my mind.

Of you who fathered me, I know
Not more than I am told;
I did not seek your inner self
When I was three years old.

Only the lines your pencil wrote
In little bursts of shine
Remain to tell me that your thoughts
Ranged the same roads as mine.

(August, 1964)

Only a Child, Alone

At the bottom of the slatted iron fire escape there was a place
where we used to play, not together but singly and at different
times, because it was a secret and hidden place, enclosed on
three sides by the back of our house and the house adjacent.
Hardly any sun ever reached this place, and when it did it was
like a pale finger that crept down between the buildings to touch
a spot on the ground without warming it. No grass grew here.
The earth was hard-packed and damp, and it had a smell like
potatoes going to sprout. In places it was dusted with a thin fuzz
of yellow-green moss that you could scrape away with the edge
of last year's Popsicle stick stained grey from winter. Here and
there were tall spindly weeds with a rank smell, and tiny white
specks, with tinier yellow centres, for flowers. The only other
thing that grew here was camomile.

You were alone and secret in this place, even if it was blazing
noon out in the street. Above you, washing flapped in the breeze,
and sometimes something wet and clammy came tumbling
down through tree branches to land beside you on the muddy
ground – a pair of white cotton panties you might lift gingerly on
the end of a stick and heave aside. Sometimes a woman came
out to bang a mop against a railing, and down floated dust
bunnies, dreamy as snow. Out of open kitchen windows came
the sounds and smells of other people's houses: a baby crying, a
radio playing, the whine of a vacuum cleaner, a mother singing
or scolding, clatter of cutlery, smell of tomato soup, smell of
floorwax.

Sometimes I think my love of cities is actually the love of
such small, enclosed spaces, glimpsed from bus windows, from
other people's balconies, through dusty screen doors: spaces that

*breathe a promise which has no words but can be heard in the
wind that rises before the first summer thunderstorm, or in the
first night rains of early spring. Spaces that make a harmony out
of an old tree trunk, grey wooden sheds and stairways slanting
between walls of buildings, a balcony-rail graced with
geraniums, a line of washing, a black iron spiral of fire escape,
the dance of leaf-shadows on a red brick wall. Sometimes a
squirrel, a cat – the ambiance of cats, their musk in the sparse
weeds at the base of the presiding tree. These spaces are cool and
dank, they are shafts, well-like, in which – one can sense – the
pull of generations has been caught forever in an eddy, to swirl
there like a movement of air, like a silent chord, born again and
again out of its own echo.*

*One glimpses these spaces in passing but does not enter them.
Only a child, alone, may play there, singing a private song,
squatting under the fire escape and scraping at the dirt with half
of a broken clothes-peg to uncover sacred relics: a blackened
penny; a scratched marble; pieces of blue glass, of green glass; a
rubber wheel off a Dinky toy, or maybe the hollow body of the
truck itself, packed tight with clay-like mud; Coke bottle caps,
caked with the same mud; a large button, a small button, their
holes mud-plugged; a mateless earring; a key that will open
nothing.*

A Solstice Rose

I prop my drooping rose
(its toppled head
hung on the limp stalk
of its spent neck)

first, on a wishful finger:
tilting the vase this way
and that, for a point
of balance that won't endure;

then, on a twist-tie's wrapped
wire, fished from a drawer
to fashion a spiral collar.
There, my dear; linger;

I've bought you a day's grace.
Drink up, stand tall. Trap
in the shady overlap
of your milky petals, some pale

December sun (its pearl
like yours, ephemeral)
as I've trapped your nodding head
awake, in a brace of metal.

Circular

The death threat in the letter that goes round
the world nine times, spreading its tentacles;
the fortune in the cookie, or the found
playing-card; the Page of Pentacles
inverted on the table; lines on the palm
or tea leaves in the bottom of a cup –
our public selves pooh-pooh without a qualm.
Our private selves are sure the game is up.

A broken mirror? Vacuum up the slivers
and think no more on it. Follow a black cat
under the nearest ladder. Shrug the shivers.
Pick up the mail that waits you on the mat:
Ignore this letter and forgo great gain.
You have been chosen. Do not break the chain.

Letter in Reply to Linda's from Yangshuo

Montreal, April 23

On the vestibule mat, your wet letter
invoking spring green in Yangshuo,
apple branches white with blossom:

It might as well be in Chinese
arriving, as it does, in a spring blizzard –
wind whirling sleet-stinging snow
to plaster the coats of walkers,
festooning our own trees in a white
too cold for fragrance.

– Only a day later, we sweep wet drifts
off the balconies, watch metal steam dry
under a warm sun. And sit outside
in our shirtsleeves in a white world,
falling water chiming all around!

Spring Song

Exhume, exhume, cold crust.
Release to gentle air
the small trapped shrubs
and rusted implements,
the rose trees wrapped
in burlap sacking. Melt around
the widowed mitten, draggled
on the ground. Lay bare
the dregs of winter.

On this the first clear-pavement day
people are dressed for yesterday.
See how our boots encumber
feet that would levitate
after our helium heads
on wafts of steam!
– our boots grown bootless,
weighing us down
like moon boots.

Cipher

So a day begins with a dead
bird on the stoop, a gift
from the cat. Poor
eyeless inert bundle,
still warm, poor scrap.
A featherweight. So a day
begins with burying a bird
in a far corner
of the front yard,
make of it what you will.

Later, a friend's letter,
homesick on the other side
of the world: *Perhaps it is good*
to miss things. So you have
what to desire.

And later still:
On the way to the store
you pass a woman weeping
in a parked car.

Random grains in the day's sieve.
Nothing adds up.
The signs are what they are.

The Face

Turn a corner, tiptoe into June,
and, waiting at the bus stop, witness
this small mystery:
the heavy halves of a broken face
of chalk-white plaster, handed out a window
carefully,
        one by one,
                to two
waiting upon the lawn
with upstretched arms:
a man and woman, leaving in their wake
dark footprints in the dewy grass
as they turn from the window, walk away
cradling the separate pieces of their charge.

Wonder whose likeness was the broken face,
how broken, and by whom,
and who and whence the bearers of its halves,
bound where? And why the deed
transacted through a window?

– Wonder; then cease.
Take up your skein of interrupted thought.

The bus is coming, and the sun flares hot
around the edges of a pewter cloud
it soon will burn through.

You'll never know, nor do you need to know.
A grace resides in mysteries like these.

Salvages

Among the beachstones, some
wink at you, sunwet.

Rocks you would not think
of pocketing, if you met them dry,
ride home knocking against your thigh.

Next day, ranged upon the sill
they are nothing if not dull,
these mute lumps – grainy and grey.

Where are the glints that caught your eye?
What made you pick them?

Lick them.

Poem

A poem is a small machine
to move the heart.
Set it at 'start'
and let it shift the mind
from one plane to another.
When the heart's a heavy stone
the mind can't hope
to lift alone,
slip it between.
The poem is a lever.

Rattled

Something has jarred loose in the mind.
An old grief, like a marble rolling around
in an empty drawer – hitting the sides
and rolling again, making a hollow
wavering aimless scrawl of sound.

A winter fly, trapped between windowpanes,
wakens to buzz the dusty glass.

The heart has its stops and starts.
Sometimes you wake with the taste
of death in your mouth,
like bitter silver.

Moments on a Balcony

He says, 'These birds
sometimes fill the air like confetti,
a handful of confetti, tossed up
or tossed down.'

And her eye too has tracked
their flocking, but her head
is elsewhere utterly,
with the uncles on Arlington,
and the scuttlebutt from Nantucket.

They sit in a swoon of linden.
It is the midpoint
of the year's midsummer light.
They yawn beneath the awning.

She says, 'Oh, but I liked
the backlit lambs, their haloes.'
She remembers a dream then,
a dream of running for cover.

It darkens above her
like an approaching storm.
She thinks, *We are not young any more.*

The birds twist up again
like a scarf of black chiffon.

Annual

The yearbooks are out today, with the ink
barely dry on their gleaming pages,
the faint puke-smell of the new bindings.

On the bus, shagged and curly heads converge over
the disappointing spread of candid shots
on centre facing pages – random snaps
where everyone who matters is blurred or too tiny
or was looking the wrong way when the shutter clicked,

and after they've each checked out their own
and each other's mug shots, and those of an acknowledged
hunk or two ('Too bad guys, doesn't he look
retarded in that picture?') you can almost
feel the thought rise: *Is that it then?*
four years reduced to this thin, already-
thumbed album of postage-stamp grins
and badly cropped halftones in a grey collage
of moments no one remembers?

Tomorrow they'll tote it back to school though,
to whip from their graffitied bags
in the mandatory feeding frenzy
for autographs – everyone's, please.
Now and only for a second
is let-down palpable in the air,
like a half-formed bubble wobbling
on the wand, then sucked back.
In a moment they'll swarm to their feet

and pull the bell (each at least once)
as they stream for the door, flashing shoulder-
freckles, wrist-bangles, navels like thumbprints in
June-white midriffs, damp wisps at the nape
wafting back a fine vapour
of girl sweat and spray cologne.

Riveted

It is possible that things will not get better
than they are now, or have been known to be.
It is possible that we are past the middle now.
It is possible that we have crossed the great water
without knowing it, and stand now on the other side.
Yes: I think that we have crossed it. Now
we are being given tickets, and they are not
tickets to the show we had been thinking of,
but to a different show, clearly inferior.

Check again: it is our own name on the envelope.
The tickets are to that other show.

It is possible that we will walk out of the darkened hall
without waiting for the last act: people do.
Some people do. But it is probable
that we will stay seated in our narrow seats
all through the tedious dénouement
to the unsurprising end – riveted, as it were;
spellbound by our own imperfect lives
because they are lives,
and because they are ours.

Did You Ever

In the thicket of conversation suddenly
the glint of an expression fallen from fashion,
Did you ever! like the cry of a rare bird
from the heart of the wood that is one's childhood,
from the heartwood. Or like any sound lost
to the past – clop of horses' hooves
on city pavement, hoot of a passing train.

That it should bring to mind (why *this*, of all
things possible?) the mother-of-pearl clasp
that fastened your granny's pale-blue cardigan
at the throat – cashmere gone limp and thin
from wear and washings, the sleeves cut off
above the elbow, frugal salvage after moths'
soft ravage and the fray of cuffs.

The say of a day long gone,
like a singular sighting
of a vanished species –
its flicker across the present.

To a Daughter in Her Twentieth Year

Whose woods these are I think I know.
These are your woods. They are not mine at all.
These woods of yours have nothing to do
    with me, your mother. They are a green wall
you have walked into, or passed through.
    They are your own green world. Within, you fall
and rise and fall again, you go
    crashing through bracken, and I hear you call,
I hear you like a panicked doe
    thrashing in thicket – you, who have grown tall
and turned from what you took for true
    till recently on faith. And it is a still, small

voice, that tells me now whose woods these are.
These woods are yours. I have my own in store.

Baggage

Born at flood-tide, I was a child
of makeshift houses. I have learned
to improvise, to lean my weight
against the slant of a warped floor,
to live without artefacts. It is for you,
my children, that I have gone out
to find the baggage
and I have dragged the baggage
up the stairs, onto the front porch.
It is there, just outside the door:
your heritage, children,
brought back from the flood.

I am tired, the baggage is
waterlogged, it is heavy, I have
dragged it a long way. Enough!
I have grown used to bare rooms,
they ask nothing of me.
The flood that robbed me
of my baggage, robbed me also
of my need for it. I shall go out
on the same tide, dispossessed
but singing: we lose
what we lose. I have lived
in interesting times.

Enough that I can wave a hand
at the front porch and say
There it is, it's yours,

I have salvaged what I could.
There is the treasure I was denied
and the curse I was spared: unopened,
I pass it on.
My mother remembers
there are beautiful things inside.
I believe her, but I am tired.
It is for you to bring it inside.
It is for you to unpack.

The Orchestre du Conservatoire
Rehearses in Salle St-Sulpice

Come with me now: round to the side entrance
and down the marble stairs,
past the Sunday dwarf who guards the *Vestiaire*,
to the basement hall with its faint smell
of a scooped-out pumpkin – quickly, come,

we are late, you see – already
the bows are sliding up and down
under the dim spotlights where smoke
from morning cigarettes collects to hang
like a blue island on the musty air …

You can write your name in dust
on the wooden seats of the fold-down chairs
where the hinged cases lie open
like empty carapaces, lined in old plush
motheaten blue or threadbare red

blackened by tarnish from silver keys
or dandruffed by rosin. On the *scène*
the *chef d'orchestre*, haloed by wild hair,
bohemian in a new red flannel shirt
points at the brass with trembling stick,

and the bell of a French horn, raised on cue,
gleams a reply. One long golden note
hurts into being, drawn out pure till he
clips it off with a flick – then drops into a
mincing squat, hissing

Pianissimo!

(and beyond the heavy drapes, out
on the snowy street, making moan,
the hooded pigeons promenade
to a solemn bonging of bells.)

The Plunge

Margaret's flute flashes in the sun
that slants in through the studio window
over her shoulder, where her cornsilk hair

falls straight and shining. Margaret's lips
hover above the tone-hole of her flute
in a perpetual half-smile that seems to dance

in place, on that curved edge of plated silver,
after the antics of her nimble fingers.
When she rests (one toe inside her shoe

counting the measures to her next entry)
her head is tilted in an air
of listening reverie, her gentle brow

shadowed with just the whisper of a crease
till with an energetic nod (her laughing lips
poised for the plunge) she launches

gaily into the next bright breathy phrase.
– Carried by currents, trusting of the tune.
Margaret's flute flashes in the sun.

Microcosms

A magic *O*, to match the *O*
of the child's mouth;
a rainbow film, to catch the *hoo*
of the child's breath,
and lo! A shining globe, new-made.
Compact of soap and water, air
and light. There it hangs,
and at its bottom hangs
a drop of concentrated froth,
vestige of closure, souvenir
of the departure from the wand.
Navel and parachute.

Now with a waft of air
the bubble floats clear
of the balcony rail – hovers there –
reflecting tinily in its roundness
all it will soon give up
with its borrowed breath:
June foliage, the house,
and the house's own sky-
reflecting windows, many small panes
containing clouds and blueness.

Suddenly it pops!
Down drops the bead
of sudsy spume, released;
a bit of spittle on the wind,
gone in a wink.

Then the child's voice, small
with surprise: *Mummy. I think
I saw the bubble's soul.*

Windfall

A dream like a shell
washed up at your feet
and whole. Luminous,
numinous. You lie quietly
looking at the ceiling.

How to preserve its shape
against the light's
incursion? (Don't blink.)
Paper and ink – lose no time,
get it on paper.

After all it's your dream,
no one can call it stealing.
Hardly any need
to dress it up. It is its
own glass slipper.

Two Conversations about Poetry

i

The bees come up from Sodom
in the autumn. They wear pink hats
and carry little umbrellas …. do you
know that poem? he asks her
over breakfast, on the balcony,
deadpan, in the beautiful hard early
morning light of August ending. His
eyes taking her measure over the rim
of his coffee mug – calm as a lizard's
eyes. *e.e. cummings*, he adds slyly, but a
second too late: sometimes she does know
when her leg is being pulled.
Oh ho ho, she says.

ii

What is the *about* of your poems, he
wants to know – what is the shall we say
boogie of this one?

A poem is an object, is what
she tells him. There is no
about of it. Like a quilt,
like a kite – but made of words.
If there is a boogie, it is
of no consequence, it is quite
beside the point. Does it warm you?
Does it fly?

He doesn't buy that
for a minute.

Ponte Vedra

It was lizard hour in the lanai.
The lizards were running back and forth
on the white ceramic tiles, under the white
wrought-iron chairs. The smell of the earth
rose evening-deep from the corner beds.
It was a Roman hour
of twilit clarity: air
like white wine, the palm fronds
darkening in sky's apricot afterglow,
white villas across the lagoon
revealing as in a dream the mathematical
purity of their lines and spacing.

It was an hour free of sediment
or sentiment. Pure as a baby's yawn.
Without price. A thing in itself,
like a marble egg, reflecting
things-in-themselves. It did not
want for anything. It was not
to be bought or sold, and nothing
needed to be bought on its account.
In it nothing was quite real, but things
were as they seemed. A languid hour
in the lanai on the lagoon.
Florida, redeemed.

Getting In Deeper

You were about to read from your
new collection of poems, entitled *Four
Deepsea Dives of the English Language*, when
someone in the front row stood up and
accused you in front of everyone! It was
a fairly serious charge, too: *You knew
about the body in the basement.*
Well. There was only one thing to do.

Holding your head high you quietly
walked off the stage, straight out the
side exit and down the hall until
you saw a room marked 'Ladies', where you knew
you could discreetly disburden yourself
of your large wad of Bazooka gum.
This took care of your main worry. Some
college girls seemed to be watching, though.

It wasn't the time to linger and admire
the naked babies rolling like porpoises
in the row of aquariums that were really
toilet-tanks. This was just as well,
because you realized all at once that your
train would be leaving in ten minutes!
You ran like hell and just made it. What a relief.
Only it seemed you had forgotten your Chinese flute...

Afterthought

O – I should never
have let the vet
cut the cat, should not
have let him open her – no, no –
the reproach of that white
shaved belly with its soft
stitched dent!
       a belly meant
to pillow tiny kneading, tiny
smacking sounds, and she
rolled on her back to give
best purchase, purring up a storm,
eyes half shut in a swoon
of ecstasy –

O what came over me, what
mad excess of mean sanity,
ever to let the vet
cut the cat?

Surprised

A bird tries on a different tune,
a winter bird on a sunny bough
in a tree set wildly a-sway
by a stiff wind on a winter's day:

a bird buffeted in his usual tree,
surprised into altering his melody –
buffing a new song to a fine shine
as a way of keeping his footing

   – though the old song would equally have done,
songs being songs. Here are two great things:
to strike one note in ever-changing light,
or to try on a new tune amid sameness;

whichever way, to embrace change, celebrate –
to change the song or sing the changes.

Change

The maple in first blush,
like an apple on the edge
of reddening – so it begins;

Later, something pulls
the leaves down, sky floods
the forks of trees.

Spendthrift, the little linden
looses the last of its gold,
clinkless coins for the wind
to hoard in heaps;

Diehard, the willow clings to its
wintry slips of yellow,
fistfuls of an obsolete
currency, see them flutter.

Carpet of crispness! hard rain
of acorns, spiky
chestnut-hulls!
Season of loss and store –

The squirrels, grown plush,
zip up stuffed tummies
for winter.

The Twentieth, Ending

These are the year's last yellow leaves – in sum
the year's, the decade's, and the century's
last yellow leaves – O look upon them, these,
last yellow leaves of the millennium!
See how they blaze, like any year's last leaves,
in the late benedictions of the sun;
then how they fly up at a gust, undone,
to blizzard their undoing past the eaves.

So fly the years, the centuries themselves
like Goldengrove unleaving; all their storm
and glory, pressed and bound on dusty shelves
to freeze the blood and keep the marrow warm
of one who comes tomorrow – one who cleaves
to the old ways, and turns the yellowed leaves.

Churlish Countdown

Let the year change
with a digital click, and let us please
get on with life. A new millennium,
big deal. We just want it over,
the big deal, that is; and the party too,
we want the party over,
we never asked for a party,
nobody's in the mood for one.
Besides, who's going to clean up the mess?

The thousand years gone by
don't feel like much to dance about
when all's said and done.
Some good stuff in there, no doubt,
but more to make you good and sick.
Enough, anyway, to say: Spare us the paean.
Let the year, like other years, go out
with a digital click.
Call it an aeon.

A Confused Heart

All right, I admit it, I'm to blame,
it's on account of me
the Messiah doesn't come;

I am the blip on the screen,
the cold spot, the dark area you see
with indefinite borders, moving sluggishly

crabwise, with a density all its own,
unabsorbed, indissoluble; the clot
in the body politic – that's me,

accountable by myself (though not alone)
for the tarrying footfall, for our
continuing bad name:

because of my imperfect faith,
my ritual omissions, my mistakes in form,
my little games of nor-care-I,

because I am stiff-necked, and push
the quarrel with God one step too far,
preferring to do the thing my way

rather than not at all (unable
to play by the rules to save my life,
unwilling to drop the ball) –

because I confuse having a part
with holding apart, and star with shield;
because I will always pause

in my studies along the road, to say
How fair is that field,
how fine is that tree;

because I have made strange fire
again and again, and lived,
and the earth has not swallowed me.

Tisha B'Av During Negotiations on the Status of Jerusalem

I fasted while the Temple burned,
and in the late afternoon, covered my eyes
with an airline blindfold
to stem migraine, and slept an hour.

At twilight my eyes were opened.
I rose from my couch, read Lamentations,
then ate a small meal, gratefully,
but the headache lingered

like the smell of char drifting across
that sacked city, up into the ring
of surrounding hills, and on up
through the centuries.

The Unharmed

War has a long wake. Waves of two long wars
washed us up slapped and gasping, upside down,
into our here and now:
their storm-swell, slow subsiding,
our cradle rocking. What could we know
of what it smashed before?
Cushioned upon its gentled lap and slap
we doze awake, ride high and dry
the caulked cocoons of our unearned lives.

We are the generation spared,
bubbles of a rolling boil
whose heat we never felt,
coddled and cosseted and silver-spooned,
unmindful of our luck – to have been dealt
so charmed a hand, in an unforgiving world!
– So we stand, the unharmed,
mute by the cenotaph,
reading the names of some who died.

We are the message in the bottle
bobbing unopened on the ebbing tide:
a cipher on a slip
of paper curled
around the Reason Why.
We are the writing that stayed dry,
and cannot read itself.

November 11, 2000. For Dr F. W. Lundell (d. March 5, 2001)

Circa 2000

Imperatives of Get and Spend
still ruled the day.

The sunlight was different.
It had been whitening
over a decade, year by year.
No one talked of this.

The ubiquitous young
of the city, shorn and pierced,
cluttered the bases of the monuments.
In your face, they said. *In your dreams.*

There was the small racket of a
toybox being dumped
or combed – this was the
foreground noise. Behind it,
distant sirens.

People were having a
fulsome interlude with a
lady poet, but they still
watched tv.
Some booed the anthem.
There were blessings
circulating privately.

Wireborne viruses took
the spotlight. Meanwhile, as wreckers
arrived to gut the derelict sanatorium,
White Plague was making a
quiet comeback.

Superstition was collecting
like a brown mist in ditches
by the side of the road.
Jerusalem was up for grabs again.

Some of us had our ear
to the wall. We were a
mind willing to change.

A Vision of the Future

After the Oil Wars, the big boys
laid waste the fields.

The usual things got said
by poets, pundits, and the common man
left to pick up the pieces.
In a room with a drawn shade
a girl stood gazing at her own
face in a cracked mirror.
Could that be her?
Does the world just go on, then?

Yes: on and on.
And in the early morning sun
a woman sits upon a stair
of broken stone
in the middle of what was once a lawn
in front of a burnt house.
She clutches a handbag, staring straight ahead
as a small wind speaks round her ears.

Day

A single chair in an otherwise empty room.
It is a statement of a kind.
It is an invitation, perhaps.
A cry of abandonment, perhaps.
Something for the room to align itself around.
Molecules of air displaced by its woodenness.
Light falling on/glancing off its woodenness.
Its placement in relation to the walls
And windows. Its angle in relation
To the room's square corners.

Shadow of chair slanting across square
Of sun on floor: black stripes
Of rungs eclipsing, fanning out again.
Now swallowed by shade.
Now there again, lit
From another direction.

These are the points of reference:
Floor, ceiling, walls, windows, door. (Fixed.)
Chair. (Moveable.)
Shadow of chair.
(Moving.)

So a new day presents itself.
Come. Sit.

Time

Like the man contracted to build movie sets
and strike them a day later –
is this how God made the world?
To serve a script?
'Lights, cameras, action!'
Then, 'Cut!' again and again,
with many retakes, generation
unto generation.

Shadows shrink to nothing, reappear
and lengthen again across the set.
Finally, did we get it right?
It will have to do, time's up.
Time to call it a day.
Somewhere a team is already assembled
to begin the dismantling.
Truck's on the way.

At the end of the day, what waits
but the End of Days.

Vidui

Poetry is my firepan. In it
I offer up my smoking heart
in words that burn and give off
a sweet savour.

If this my only service
be unacceptable unto the One
Who heareth prayer, alas! what
will become of me?

Fishless

It was past prime of day.
Light was beginning to flood the sky
as a rising tide floods sand flats.
The sky became a blotter for light,
drinking it from the edges.

I wanted to hide from the day's brightness.
Brightness that tells on me,
brightness that hunts me out and
fails not to find me, a shrinking snail.
Brightness that roasts me –

It was past star wane and past
the still hour of listening. I had let
it slip away, the womb-hour; the net
once again had come up fishless.
I wanted to hide from the day's brightness.

Salve

Prickly
over a layer of old hurt
(but who isn't, at twenty?)
you antler me away –

I who can do nothing
to change the past,
daughter – can only pray
that you not harden

around your wounds, not calcify
those barbs into a shell
to baffle all access, but spare
a soft spot, like a second fontanel

over whose quiet pulsing I may hope
gently to lay my hand one day.

A Silence

My dearest uncle is gone, and I,
I see I never spoke to him
in my true voice.
I never spoke my heart,
or knocked on his.

How will I find my way
from here? The woods grow denser.
The words, too:
The words gather in density
like banks of cloud on the horizon
blocking the sunset light,
and still they spin from me,
and still
they spill like mist,
they wind like wool.

So do we darken
our own path.

Old Tune

Beat time,
beat time to the music while you can,
for no one can beat time forever.
No, in the end no one beats time.
Time beats us all,
a cold conductor.

Nothing there is that is not
by time's iron touched,
by time's cold iron
tempered in its turn.
Not any man escapes this brush.
Time's iron hold, time's icy burn.
– But in the din of dying,
what truth shines? What reveille,
in this cold branding?

Some claim to know.
Some say we cannot know.
For all, the shepherd's pipe
plays the same tune.
The rod is raised, the rod comes down.
Beat time, then, while you can.

The days rattle past with their sheep tags.
The woolly huddle of days,
the woolly blur of them,
tagged and numbered.

Hearth

Prayers, poems; candles and coloured lights
at the winter solstice; jazz
in the summer twilights – these are all
feints at the dark.
They don't fool anybody.

No sooner come of age than death
has begun to tug at our clothes
like a child demanding to be noticed,
small fist has us by the coattails
and won't let go.

Let's put on the old records
and dance. Light shuts like a fan.
But heart and earth
make hearth: our home on earth
while the heart beats.

Levels

In this city the hospitals
are on the hill, the sick look down
from their high place, upon the tortuous
peregrinations of the well,
or they look up, they gaze on the serene
procession of clouds. And theirs
is the realm between.

I think of you up there,
remote behind your allocated pane,
your porthole on the man-swarm
and eternity. No way to know
which way you're facing now,
what side you'll exit on, this time,
how much you think on it, or care.

A life is a life. What
will we make of that?
What is the real world?
Privately, no one believes
he's living in it.

We are about to begin the descent,
the voice says. We say: *I've paid my dues.*

Sunset. It is the hour when hospital windows
beam gold into the eyes
of runners on the upper avenues.

Home

The harbour of each other.
Skin to skin. Folding into each
other's limbs after
long time apart.
The quilt drawn over
our heads so we can
burrow into the good smell
of each other, then make the
good smell that we make together.
Like a bread that we bake
in the good heat of each other.

This is our little house,
you say as we lie solemnly
eye to eye (or maybe it is
I who say it) cupped hands forming
blinkers to shade our gaze.
Or: Come in to my tent, you say.

Yes. This.

Sunny Days Following a Death in Late Winter

A sun invasion.
The ground snowed under, but
this onslaught of light –
sudden, unbidden, I'm not
prepared for it.

Soon the air will be
sweet at open windows,
the watermelon smell
of melt.
No stemming it.

Now only the light
assails, itself
more than enough. Where
can I hide, too soon
besieged by spring?

Tony's Sharpening

A summer evening sound, his silver bell
summoning householders to bring
their scissors, kitchen knives, blunt blades
to sing against his whetstone.

Tony the Sharpener. He used to pass
on a bicycle, years back.
Now it's a little truck he has,
but the same sweet-toned bell

*cling-cling*s across the evening's
linden-laden air, the languid games
of after-supper children
granted a stay of bath and bed

for the red hour of afterglow
when robins pipe in the hedge.
Tony, spin your stone again,
give life back its edge.

Bell

It is the end of August, August ending.
Already the light has dropped – as the
lake's level drops in a dry season,
leaving its dark high-water mark
on the dock's once-mossy vertical.
The undergrowth has begun to die back, a
green wave receding; in its wake
the crust of things drying – flower
heads browning, twists of copper leaf
and silver fluff. (Whispers of what's
to come: the sere, austere
November dusk, wind's hiss
in the tawny ribbons of standing weeds
as the light folds down its shutters.

So will we go when our time comes, all of us,
all who are not cut down
in the waxing of our days, go in our waning:
liver-spotted, dishevelled, shedding
dull flakes of skin and silver strands of hair
on the faded carpet, on the arms of chairs,
our milky, frost-glazed eyes
mild in the gathering gloom,
but our hearts still wild.)

Now at the end of August, August ending,
as the evening drops its awning,

each city block seems to have its
resident cricket – solo, unseen –
harbinger in an unmarked garden –
pitching its silver timbrel to the
streetlamps' pearl, then sounding
and sounding a solemn pulse
across its own field of audibility
in a wide, shimmering bell of elegy.

Day Visit

He had already turned to walk away
When she looked back. And he did not look back.
The train began to inch along the track,
Then picked up speed, then left the station bay.
She stowed her knapsack on the luggage rack.
Through banks of cloud, one broad bedazzling ray
Of setting sun shone red on bales of hay
In autumn fields. She watched the land go black.

She thought she understood him: why prolong
A valediction in the afternoon –
A visit preordained to end too soon?
(She'd made the reservation to be strong.)
Why *should* he pause to wave? Proper goodbyes
Are crisp. Besides, the sun was in his eyes.

Bounty

Make much of something small.
The pouring-out of tea,
a drying flower's shadow on the wall
from last week's sad bouquet.
A fact: it isn't summer any more.

Say that December sun
is pitiless, but crystalline
and strikes like a bell.
Say it plays colours like a glockenspiel.
It shows the dust as well,

the elemental sediment
your broom has missed,
and lights each grain of sugar spilled
upon the tabletop, beside
pistachio shells, peel of a clementine.

Slippers and morning papers on the floor,
and wafts of iron heat from rumbling rads,
can this be all? No, look – here comes the cat,
with one ear inside out.
Make much of something small.

The Circle

i

A drop of wine fell upon the page
and made a soft, round pink star
there, where it dried. A focal point
for another day's dreaming
over the white field of the empty page,
the white cloth, dropped on the sere ground.

She saw a painting once: A door opening
on a moonlit winter landscape.
On the threshold, a single shoe,
pointing outward. Its mate
tipped on its side, a foot or two behind.

It is like that, the white cloth.
A snow field, untrodden.

ii

She unpacks a new day
from its shipping crate,
another crated day. It blinks at her first
through the slats. They blink at each other.
It is new and not new.
She likes a mix of dim daylight
and lamplight, like a mixed drink;
to get the mix just right.

Sometimes it is as though
she needs a new window.
She wants to make herself a window.
No, she thinks. What I need is to learn
how to *be* a window. To give onto the world,
be through-shine. (She wants to make her
self a window.)

iii

A drop of wine dried upon the page
and left a pink star, a rose window, there.
Something for her to wrap her nib around.
Something for her to dream on.
She draws a circle round it now.

This is the work of her hands:
she keeps a tally of days,
a ledger of dreams. It is all
a little nebulous. Sometimes
she fears herself pretender,
even to her own throne.

Nothing for it then
but idiot faith.
That keeps her going.

To N, *in absentia*

I do not know how you went out of my life
or when exactly. The leaves of the Norway maple
are beginning to turn yellow, fall has come.
I last saw you on an evening at the end of July
but I think you were already gone then,
I think by then you had been gone for a long time.

And so it seems meaningless to count the days
yet still I count them, August, September,
October now half over, terrible days,
and I do not know where you are
or when I may have news of you again.
But I remember as if yesterday the day
you came out of my body into this world,
a fine splash in full midsummer, a small cry
like the meow of a Siamese cat,
your eyes wide open and looking all around;
remember how in the early hours of that morning,
before you arrived, I heard pass down our street
(as I had heard each morning of that summer
of my thirtieth year) the clopping sound
of a lone horse pulling a calèche,
his sleepy driver bound for the road
that climbs Mount Royal's slope.

No one can take away that morning
or the exactness of its place in time.
I go there often.
I visit it like a temple.

Here/ There

What is the meaning of place?
What does it mean to say, *This
is my own, my native land*, or
Here were my forefathers born,
or: *On this spot the house once stood* ... ?

      Winged things exist that cross
      great distances to lay
      eggs on the self-same tree
      where they were hatched.

      A cat just wants somewhere
      warm to lie down.

      And young folk? To get away –
      as far away as they can
      from wherever they began.

Sometimes it is a wish to stand
upon a site that stirred
imagination from afar – some land
storied and pictured,
              or an elsewhere
remembered, but by someone else –

(as I am sometimes homesick
for the *shtetl* I never saw,
whose denizens in turn
yearned for Jerusalem ...)

    An accident of history, our birthplace
    binds us – early though we leave it.
    Binds us by name, by law,
    if by no more.

    Whatever our final shore,
    it is the childhood home
    old age remembers.

Get thee forth and *Get thee back*
are the beginnings of two stories
good for a lifetime,
               as wandering
is only wandering
in relation to somewhere left behind
or yet to find.

The High Meadows

As the afternoon shadows of hills
move across each other's faces
so do the decades cast shadows:
deep shadows have flooded whole folds
of the time that's left me,
extinguishing the light once cupped
in their embrace, each space
its own measure of warm gold
doused now, put to sleep,
smoking green-blue, blue-
black, a whisper
of haze and fade.
How few are the places left
that the sun has not abandoned!
the high meadows! I will run
to gain them while the light lasts,
run and run uphill,
a late sprint
with night's cool breath
at my shoulder.

Acknowledgements

My thanks to the editors of the following journals in which these poems first appeared:

Arc: 'The High Meadows'. *Books in Canada:* 'Sunny Days Following a Death in Midwinter', 'Circular', 'Day Visit'. *Boulevard:* 'Annual'. *The Hudson Review:* 'Tony's Sharpening'. *Maisonneuve:* 'A Vision of the Future'. *The Malahat Review:* 'Day', 'Fishless', 'Getting In Deeper', 'Two Conversations about Poetry', 'Bounty', 'The Orchestre du Conservatoire Rehearses in Salle St-Sulpice'. *Michigan Quarterly Review:* 'Only a Child, Alone'. *The New Quarterly:* 'Poem', 'Hearth', 'Levels', 'Circa 2000'. *The North American Review:* 'Moments on a Balcony', 'A Solstice Rose'. *Parchment:* 'Baggage', 'Tisha B'Av During Negotiations on the Status of Jerusalem', 'Vidui'. *Poetry:* 'A Confused Heart', 'Ponte Vedra', 'The Unharmed'. *Quarterly West:* 'Cipher', 'Salvages'. *Slope:* 'Letter in Reply to Linda's from Yangshuo'. *The Threepenny Review:* 'Riveted', 'Did You Ever'.

'The Twentieth, Ending' was first published as a broadside in an edition of 50, by Delirium Press, Montreal.

I am grateful to the Conseil des Arts et des Lettres du Québec and to the Canada Council for the Arts for support at different stages in the completion of this body of work.

Special thanks to my first readers: Marc Plourde, Bruce Taylor, Don Coles, and Eric Ormsby.

Robyn Sarah was born in New York City to Canadian parents, and has lived for most of her life in Montreal. Her poetry began appearing in Canadian literary magazines in the early 1970s, while she completed studies in philosophy at McGill University and music at the Conservatoire du Québec. The author of several previous poetry collections and two collections of short stories, she is also an essayist whose writing has appeared on both sides of the border in such publications as *The Threepenny Review, New England Review, Books in Canada,* and *The New Quarterly.*